Action!

Movement in Art

by Anne Civardi

HODDER
Wayland

An imprint of Hodder Headline Limited

Titles in this series:
Action! Movement in art
Families: Relationships in art
Look At Me! Self-Portraits in art
Place and Space: Landscapes in art
Sculpture: Three dimensions in art
Telling Tales: Stories in art

For more information about this series
and other Hodder Wayland titles, go to
www.hodderwayland.co.uk

Series concept: Ruth Thomson
Series Consultant: Erika Langmuir
Editor and Picture Research: Margot Richardson
Designers: Rachel Hamdi and Holly Mann

Text copyright © Anne Civardi 2005

The right of Anne Civardi to be identified as the author of this
Work has been asserted by her in accordance with the
Copyright, Designs and Patents Act 1988.

British Library Cataloguing in Publication Data
Civardi, Anne
Action!: movement in art. - (Artventure)
1.Motion in art - Juvenile literature 2.Art appreciation -
Juvenile literature
I.Title
701.8

ISBN 0 7502 45689

Printed in China

The publishers would like to thank the following for permission
to reproduce their pictures:
Page 1 © Archivo Iconografico, S.A./CORBIS; 4-5 © Archivo
Iconografico, S.A./CORBIS; 6 Transparency courtesy Agency
Photographique de la Réunion des Musées Nationaux, Paris
© Photo CNAC; 7 Museum of Modern Art, New York,
USA/www.bridgeman.co.uk; 8–9 © Archivo Iconografico,
S.A./CORBIS; 10-11 © Historical Picture Archive/CORBIS
(Photographer: Philip de Bay); 12 Photograph by Jacques
Henri Lartigue © Ministère de la Culture - France/AAJHL;
13 © National Gallery Collection; By kind permission of the
Trustees of the National Gallery, London/CORBIS; 14 © ARS,
NY and DACS, London 2005/ National Gallery of Art,
Washington DC, USA/www.bridgeman.co.uk; 15 © Hans
Namuth Ltd; 16 © DACS 2005/Albright Knox Art Gallery,
Buffalo, New York, USA/www.bridgeman.co.uk; 17 Hulton
Archive; 18-19 M C Escher's 'Sky and Water 1' © 2004 Cordon
Art BV - Baarn - Holland. All rights reserved; 20 The Art Institute
of Chicago; 21 musée Rodin/ADAGP, Paris, photograph by
Adam Rzepka; 22-23 Mattioli Collection, Milan,
Italy/www.bridgeman.co.uk; 24-25 © ADAGP, Paris and DACS,
London 2005/akg-images; 26 © L & M SERVICES B.V.
Amsterdam 20040507; 27 © Munch Museum / Munch -
Ellingsen Group, BONO, Oslo, DACS, London 2005 /Photo ©
Munch Museum (Svein Andersen/Sidsel de Jong 2004).

weblinks

For more information about
movement in art, go to
www.waylinks.co.uk/series/
artventure/action

Contents

Words in **bold** can be found in the glossary

The art of movement

Artists use many different tricks and techniques to capture movement in their paintings or sculptures. They may use strong lines, sharp angles or quick, bold brush strokes to suggest energy or speed. **Blurred** or **distorted** shapes and certain **poses** or colours also help to bring art alive.

On the move

Georges Seurat, a French artist, worked in the nineteenth century. His picture of a lively circus scene is made up of circles, spirals and ovals. Look at how he leads your eye around the painting in a ring of movement. This circular motion adds to the action and lends a happy, carefree feeling to the painting.

- What is the first thing you notice in Seurat's picture? Does it appear to move?
- What colour has the artist used more than any other? What effect does this give?
- Do you think it took Seurat a long time or a short time to paint this picture? (It is 1.85 metres high and 1.52 metres wide.) Remember his style of painting.

Seurat used different shades of bright red and yellow for the circus ring and the performers. This has captured the joy and excitement of the spectacle. The more muted tones of darker yellow and violet make the background appear much calmer and quieter.

Making a point

Seurat invented a way of painting tiny little dots of pure colour, often red, yellow or blue, next to each other. From a distance, these colours seem to mix together, making them look bright and vibrant. This method of painting is called **'pointillism'**.

❑ Georges Seurat, **The Circus (detail)**

▶ The stillness of the upright audience and the horizontal lines of the seats contrast with the unbalanced diagonal line of the ballerina on horseback. This makes the performers seem even more lively.

▶ Look at how the positions and poses of the horse, ballerina and the acrobat make them look as if they really are dancing, balancing, galloping and tumbling.

▶ Follow the circle of movement from the clown's right hand along his scarf, around the ringmaster and the acrobat, down the ballerina, all the way to the tip of the horse's hooves and back to the clown's left hand.

❑ Georges Seurat, **The Circus**, 1890-91

Streaks and swirls

- How many riders, horses and lions can you spot?
- What do you think happened next?
- How does Delacroix's painting make you feel?

❑ Eugene Delacroix
**La Chasse aux Lions
(The Lion Hunt)**
1854

The artists who painted these two pictures both used bold, bright colours and swirling brush strokes to create a sense of dramatic motion and **mood** in their paintings.

A startling sketch

This painting by Delacroix, in the mid-nineteeth century, manages to capture the terror in the horses' eyes and the riders' fear as they are attacked by ferocious lions. The vibrant, swirling colours twist and turn, adding to the chaos and panic of the scene.

Streaks of emotion

When he painted the scene on the right, the Dutch painter, Vincent van Gogh, was in hospital in France being treated for mental illness that tormented and terrified him.

The artist was interested in using colour and vigorous lines to suggest different emotions and moods. He seems to be expressing the feelings of anguish, fear and confusion he had inside him at the time.

❏ Vincent van Gogh
Starry Night
1889

Swirling sky

The sky in Van Gogh's picture is filled with an enormous spinning moon and huge rotating yellow stars. The swirling clouds appear to be rolling uncontrollably across the picture, while the dark flame-like cypress tree twists forlornly upwards into the stormy sky. This sense of intense movement contrasts with the quiet vertical and horizontal lines of the sleepy village below.

Dabs and dashes

Claude Monet, another French artist working in the late nineteenth century, painted this striking picture of a festival in Paris looking down from a nearby window. Like other **Impressionist** painters, he liked to create pictures of things he could see with his own eyes. He managed to capture the effects of movement and light on outdoor scenes of everyday life by dabbing strokes of paint quickly on to his **canvas**.

Monet's magic

The lively, vibrant colours convey the noise and thrill of the crowd. Monet could create whatever mood he wanted with a dash of colour and a quick stroke of his brush. To give the painting as much movement as possible, Monet did not use any outlines or details.

❑ Claude Monet
The Rue Montorgueil, Paris, 30 June 1878
1878

Fluttering French flags

The dabs and dashes of red, white and blue paint on either side of the painting represent hundreds of French flags waving in the wind. To suggest that they are flapping vigorously, Monet has painted some of the flags slightly blurred.

A lively crowd

A huge crowd of people bustle in the street below the flags. The artist has dabbed tiny strokes of white paint on the people to make it look as though the sun is shining down on them. Notice how much darker the shadows are.

☐ Claude Monet, **The Rue Montorgueil, Paris, 30 June 1878**, (details)

Look closely at the picture.
- Are all the flags painted in the French colours of red, white and blue?
- If the painting suddenly came alive, what sounds would you hear? Describe the different noises.
- Half-close your eyes – see how the picture really does look as if it is moving.

Paris in perspective

The buildings, flags and people get smaller and smaller as they get further away down the crowded Paris street. This gives a feeling of distance and depth known as **perspective**. Monet managed to continue the sense of movement and excitement as far as the eye can see.

Lively lines

Artists can suggest mood and motion by the direction and shape of the lines they paint in their pictures.

Wavy lines

Look at the sweeping, curved lines Hokusai, a Japanese artist, has used to create the huge, tumbling wave in this **woodcut print**.

Curved lines, like these, give a sense of movement. **Diagonal** lines are action lines, as well.

Quiet lines

The artist has not used any horizontal or vertical lines. These are calm lines that give pictures a feeling of stillness and balance.

❑ Katsushika Hokusai, **The Great Wave off Kanagawa from the series '36 Views of Mt.Fuji'**, *about 1830-32*

❑ Katsushika Hokusai
The Great Wave off Kanagawa (detail)

Mini mountain

This picture is one of a series of thirty-six prints of Mount Fuji in Japan that Hokusai designed when he was an old man. Although the snow-capped mountain is the highest peak in the country, it looks tiny in comparison to the gigantic wave and the swelling water.

Rowing nowhere

The wave's white spray looks like lots of sharp claws ready to reach out and grab the boatmen battling their way through the rough, stormy seas. It seems impossible that they will escape the mass of water about to crash down on top of them.

- How many curved or diagonal lines can you spot in Hokusai's print?
- Look at how the dotted lines of spray under the wave lead your eye right to the top of the rolling, curling shape.
- Why do you think the artist has made the mountain so tiny?
- What does the colour of the sky suggest to you?

Wonderful woodcuts

Hokusai started as an **apprentice** in a woodcut **workshop** when he was only fifteen years old. He became a very restless man, moving home over ninety times during his life. He also changed his name several times. One of them, *Gakyo-rojin*, means 'the mad painter'. By the time he died, he had created more than 30,000 designs.

Hokusai was famous for his *ukiyoe* prints (*ukiyoe* means 'pictures of the floating world') for which he used bold colours and strong shapes. The thirty-six prints of Mount Fuji, which took him ten years to complete, are his best known. They show this magnificent mountain from all sides and in all kinds of weather.

All of a blur

An artist can give a sense of speed and drama to a picture by making some parts of it blurred.

❑ Jacques Henri Lartigue
Grand Prix de l'ACF, automobile Delage, 26 juin 1912 (First Prize of the ACF Dieppe)
1912

A fuzzy feeling

To give a sensation of speed in his photo above, Lartigue, a French photographer and painter, followed the movement of the car with his camera as it zoomed past, instead of keeping the camera absolutely still. This blurred the part of the scene – the spectators and the road – that were not moving.

The way that the racing car, half-way out of the picture, leans forwards in the direction of the movement, and the way the spectators lean backwards give a feeling of action, too.

Steaming ahead!

When the British artist Turner painted the picture opposite, steam trains, able to reach 50 miles an hour, had just been invented. As a train thundered over a bridge towards him, Turner tried to capture the excitement people must have felt at the time about its incredible speed.

To create the effects of motion and changing light in his picture, Turner did not use any outlines and painted with quick, broken brush strokes.

▼ Look at the movement and atmosphere created by Turner's slashes and streaks of colour for the clouds and stormy sky.

▼ To give an effect of changing light, the artist has used a range of colours, from grey and blue to yellow and orange.

▼ Parts of the picture (look at the right hand corner) are painted with brushstrokes of thick paint, known as **impasto**.

Out of the mist

The blurred effect adds to the power and speed of the steam train. Can't you just imagine it hurtling towards you through the driving rain and mist? This contrasts with the people in the boat below who seem to be fishing quietly in the still water.

❏ J M W Turner
**Rain, Steam and Speed –
The Great Western Railway**
about 1839-44
Turner became known as the 'painter of light' because of his interest in painting the effects of light and water in his pictures.

Splashing out

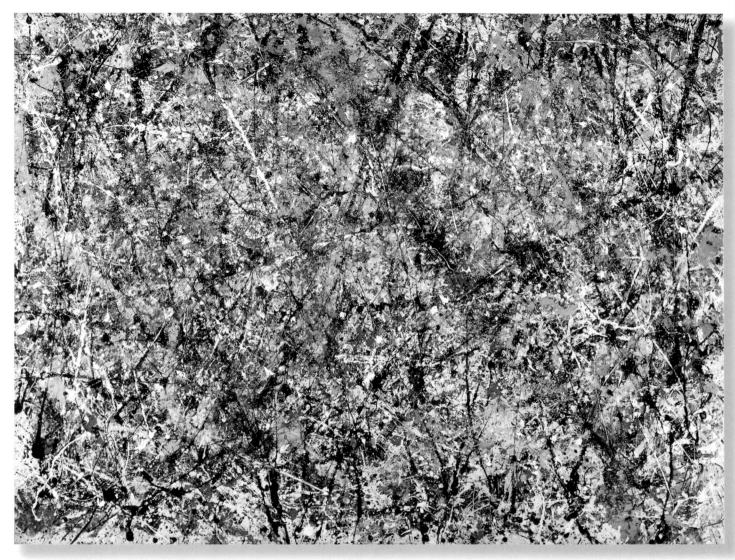

Some artists, such as the American painter Jackson Pollock, splash and pour paint on to their canvases, rather than only using brushes. This style of **abstract** art, which was most famous in the 1940s and 1950s, is called 'action painting' or '**Abstract Expressionism**'.

❑ Jackson Pollock
Lavender Mist: No 1, 1950, *1950*
This painting is huge – almost 3 metres long and over 2 metres high. Pollock used oil, enamel and aluminium paint to create it.

Action man

To create this painting, Pollock, nicknamed 'Jack the Dripper', laid a huge canvas on the ground. Then, using the movement of his whole body, he dripped, dribbled, flung and spilt paint all over it. His pictures are so busy and full of energy and movement that it is hard to keep your eye in one place.

❑ Jackson Pollock at work

Splattering with sticks

The artist used sticks, trowels, knives and brushes to splatter layers and layers of paint over his pictures. Sometimes he danced around a canvas as he worked, and once, to give it a special **texture**, he even pushed a tricycle over one of his paintings.

Indian influence

Pollock got his idea of painting in this way from the sandpaintings created by the Navajo Native American Indians in Arizona. These were usually made by sprinkling coloured sand, flowers, cornmeal and corn pollen on to the ground.

Abstract Expressionism

Action artists do not try to paint **realistic** people, animals or objects. Instead, they focus more on line, colour, texture and shape. This kind of painting is different from other types because it gives viewers a sense of the movement artists make while they are creating their pictures. It is easy to imagine Pollock dancing around as he splattered paint all over this canvas.

- What is your first impression of Pollock's abstract painting? How do you think he felt while he was painting it?
- What title would you give this picture if you had created it?
- Look at the lines in the painting. Do they suggest action or peacefulness?

Again and again

Fantastic Futurists

Giacomo Balla, an Italian artist working in the early 1900s, helped start an art movement called Futurism. **Futurists** were inspired by the power and energy of modern life. They portrayed things in motion they saw around them, such as machines, racing cars and people hurrying about. To show liveliness and speed in their art, they used overlapping images and repeated lines and shapes.

❏ Giacomo Balla
Dynamism of a Dog on a Lead
1912

- What clue tells you that the dog seems happy to be out?
- How has the artist painted the dog's leash to suggest movement?
- Why do the lines Balla has painted on the ground help convey movement?

Speedy shapes

In this famous painting by Balla, you can not only sense the little dog's excitement at being out for a walk, but you can also see how fast he has to scurry along to keep up with his mistress. The artist has blurred the dog's legs and the woman's feet, and painted them over and over again, to give a feeling of action.

Overlapping for action

Etienne-Jules Marey, a French scientist who lived from 1830 to 1904, was one of the first people to capture motion in photos. To create the picture below, he took several overlapping shots of a man **fencing** with a sword. Marey used the same glass plate inside the camera to capture each position. When a print was made from the plate, all the fencer's actions were on one photograph.

Gunning it

To take pictures of birds in flight, he created a photographic gun. By pressing the gun's trigger very quickly, he was able to capture twelve images. Each image, set around the edge of a glass plate, showed a different part of the birds' flight.

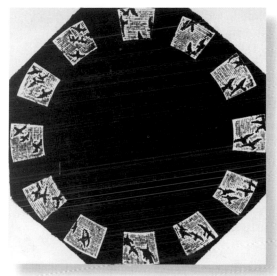

❑ Etienne Jules Marey
Gun Birds
about 1860

❑ Etienne Jules Marey
Fencing Pose
about 1890

Moving patterns

Patterns are shapes that are repeated over and over again. Some look still, while others can look as if they are flowing right across the picture.

❑ M C Escher
Sky and Water
1938

M C Escher was a twentieth-century **graphic** artist who was interested in patterns, maths and science.

Flying fish

Take a close look at his woodcut print. At first glance, all you can see is a pattern of black birds flying in the white sky with white fish swimming in the black sea below. Now let your eyes rest on the middle strip of the print. You'll see that for each of the white fish, the sea in which it is swimming is formed by the four black birds around it. Similarly, for each black bird, the sky in which it is flying is formed by the four white fish that surround it.

Notice how, as the birds get higher in the white sky, they get lighter, while the fish get darker, the deeper they are in the black sea.

❑ M C Escher
Sky and Water I (detail)

• Look at the border of lines around the print. Notice how they all move in the same direction as the birds and fish. What does this help convey?

• Focus on just the white parts of the print. How many fish can you spot? Now focus only on the black parts. How many birds can you see?

A diagonal diamond

Look at how the birds are flying and the fish are swimming in diagonal rows to form a big diamond. This creates a strong sense of movement. By changing one shape into another, the artist has managed to give the picture a feeling of energy and motion.

Off balance

The position or pose of a person in a painting or sculpture helps suggest motion. Flowing hair or floating garments also make figures come alive.

Dancing with Degas

The French painter, Edgar Degas, liked to paint ballet dancers most of all. Here, you can just imagine the ballerinas whirling across the stage in their fluffy tutus. The main dancer's pose – balancing on one leg, with her head tilted to one side and her arms outstretched – gives the **illusion** of a figure in motion. The blurred effect and the cut-off ballerina dancing out of the picture on the right both add to the sense of movement.

❏ Edgar Degas, **On the Stage**, *1876-77*

The mystery of movement

Rodin, a famous sculptor, was known for his ability to capture movement in his work. He thought that this not only brought a sculpture to life, but also gave it a mysterious quality.

A series of dancers

A few years before he died, Rodin became interested in studying dancers to capture natural movement. He drew and sculpted a series of dancers in various poses.

Moving models

Rodin did not bother portraying the body too realistically by adding things like muscles. Instead, he tried to capture the physical action of the dancers' movements. To achieve this, he asked professional dancers to perform in his **studio**, while he created quick models of them in clay.

Compare this sculpture with Boccioni's on pages 22-23.
- Which one looks more natural?
- Which one looks more graceful?
- What other differences can you spot?
- Which parts of the sculpture look distorted to you?

⊔ Auguste Rodin, **Dance Movement C**, *1910-11*

Impossible poses

Look at how successfully Rodin has captured the graceful movements of dance in this sculpture. He has managed to make us feel that the ballet dancer may topple over at any moment. We also realize that the figure will have to keep moving.

21

Bursts of energy

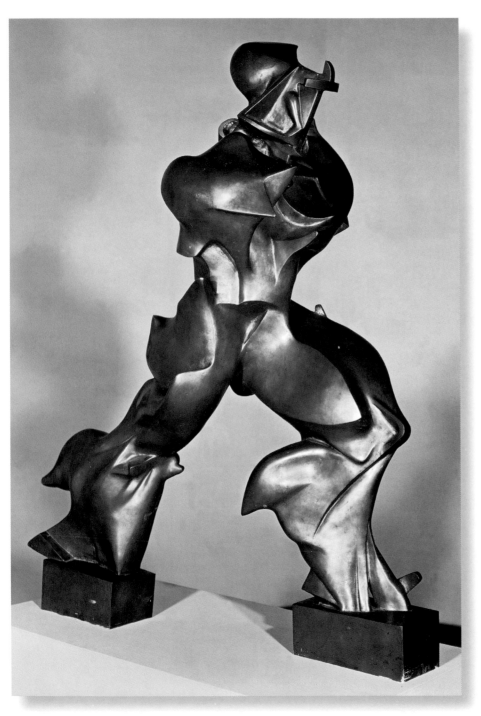

Sculptors, like painters, use special techniques to portray movement in their works of art. Sometimes they distort shapes or exaggerate them to give a feeling of speed and energy.

◀ The breastplate and helmet of Umberto Boccioni's shiny bronze figure make it look almost mechanical, like a super hero marching through space. Or perhaps it reminds you of a soldier marching off to war?

◀ Boccioni overlapped different shapes to create the figure's bulging muscles. As well as making the muscles look extra powerful, these shapes help convey a sense of motion and rhythm.

❑ Umberto Boccioni
Unique Form of Continuity in Space
1913

- Does this figure look realistic or abstract to you?
- What does it remind you of?
- Remember that sculptures are three-dimensional. That means you can view them from the front, back and sides. Think about what this figure might look like from above.

Mighty muscles

Look at how Boccioni has managed to make the figure look so powerful and strong. He has emphasized the huge, wing-like muscles to give an impression of someone striding forwards. By placing them on two small blocks, the artist leads the viewer's eyes to the feet, which seem to be making giant strides through space.

Floating through air

Although the figure looks so **dynamic** and mighty, Boccioni still makes it appear almost weightless. Notice how the muscles seem to ripple and flutter as they push aside the air in their path, just as a swimmer pushes away water. The artist has captured the way in which objects in motion relate to their surroundings as they pass.

Modern man

Like Balla (see page 16), Boccioni was a Futurist. He, too, was interested in creating works of art that represented people or objects in motion in the modern world. He once said, 'What we want to do is to show the living object in its dynamic growth ... all subjects previously used must be swept aside in order to express our whirling life of steel, of pride, of fever and of speed.'

Tricking the eye

Some artists create pictures that seem to move or change as you look at them.

❑ Victor Vasarely, **Boo,** *1978*

Op Art

Although this type of picture appears to move, the images don't really change at all: they just give the illusion of movement. In other words, they play tricks on your eyes. This kind of art, which is usually abstract, is called Op Art (Optical Art). The first examples were painted in the mid-1960s.

Fooling the brain

The Hungarian, Victor Vasarely, was one of the best known Op artists. He was interested in how people's eyes and brains work together, and how he could fool them into seeing something that wasn't actually there.

In and out

It's difficult to believe that the surface of Vasarely's painting is completely flat. It looks like two round **spheres** bouncing out. The artist managed to create this optical illusion by using line, colour and shape in extraordinary ways. Look how he has curved and distorted the lines to make the spheres bulge out, as well as to draw your eyes deep into the picture.

❏ Victor Vasarely, **Boo (detail)**

• Vasarely wanted to paint in a way that people could understand without needing special explanations. Do you think he succeeded with 'Boo'?

• Apart from the lines, what makes the two spheres look closest to us? Compare their colours to the rest of the painting.

Feelings in action

❑ Robert Delauney
**Hommage à Blériot
(Homage to Bleriot)**
1914
Delaunay's colours convey a sense of excitement as well as action. The artist was obviously happy at Louis Bleriot's great achievement.

The colours that artists use in their paintings can suggest different moods and emotions. Warm colours, such as red, yellow and orange, can make a picture feel happy and full of energy. Cool colours, such as blue, violet or green, can make it appear cold and dismal. Dark colours, such as black and purple, can make it seem scary and full of anguish.

First flight

The Frenchman Robert Delaunay's picture celebrates the first aeroplane flight over the English Channel by Louis Bleriot, in 1909. The spirals and circles of vibrant colour give the impression of a propeller whirling across the sky. Their warmth and light give the painting a feeling of joy and happiness.

Mood and emotion

Edvard Munch, a Norwegian painter, had a very difficult childhood and was plagued by psychological problems all his life. That is probably why his paintings are full of such dramatic emotion.

• What emotion do you think this person is feeling?

Look at the hollow skull-like face, wide, staring eyes, open, screaming mouth and the way the head is held in the hands.

◀ The unnatural colours of the fiery red sky, and the swirling, dark purple water both add to the menacing mood and eerie atmosphere of Munch's picture.

◀ Notice how he has used sharp angles, strong diagonal lines, distorted outlines and clashing colours to express a feeling of terror, and to suggest that something dreadful is about to happen.

❑ Edvard Munch
The Scream
1893

27

About the artists

The symbols below show the size and shape of the works shown in this book, compared with an average-sized adult.

Giacomo BALLA (page 16)

(1871-1958) Italian (Turin)
Dynamism of a Dog on a Lead, 1912
Oil on canvas, 88.75 x 108 cm
Albright-Knox Art Gallery, Buffalo, NY, USA

Other works showing movement
- *Abstract Speed + Sound*, 1913-14
  Guggenheim Museum, New York, NY, USA
- *Mercury Passing Before the Sun*, 1914
  Gianni Mattioli Collection, Venice, Italy
- *Abstract Speed – The Car has Passed*, 1913
  Tate Britain, London, UK

Umberto BOCCIONI (pages 22-23)

(1882-1916) Italian (Reggio di Calabria)
Unique Form of Continuity in Space, 1913
Bronze, 126.4 x 89 x 40.6 cm
Mattioli Collection, Milan, Italy

Other works showing movement
- *The Development of a Bottle in Space*, 1912
  Museum of Modern Art, New York, NY, USA
- *Dynamism of a Cyclist*, 1913
  Private collection
- *Dynamism of a Speeding Horse + Houses*, 1914-15
  Guggenheim Museum, New York, NY, USA

Edgar DEGAS (page 20)

(1834-1917) French (Paris)
On the Stage, 1876-77
Pastel and essence over monotype on
cream paper on board, 59.2 x 42.5 cm
Potter Palmer Collection, Art Institute of Chicago, IL, USA

Other works showing movement
- *The Rehearsal*, about 1873-78
  Fogg Art Museum, Harvard, Cambridge, MASS, USA
- *Dancer Onstage*, about 1877
  Metropolitan Museum of Art, New York, NY, USA
- *Ballet Dancers in the Wings*, about 1900
  Saint Louis Art Museum, St. Louis, MO, USA

Eugéne DELACROIX (page 6)

(1798-1863) French (near Paris)
La Chasse aux Lions (The Lion Hunt), 1854
Oil on canvas, 86 x 115 cm
Museé D'Orsay, Paris, France

Other works showing movement
- *Arab Riders on Scouting Mission*, 1862
  Hermitage Museum, Saint Petersburg, Russia
- *Christ Asleep during the Tempest*, 1850
  Metropolitan Museum of Modern Art, New York, USA
- *Arabs Skirmishing in the Mountains*, 1863
  National Gallery of Art, Washington DC, USA

Robert DELAUNAY (page 26)

(1885-1941) French (Montpellier)
Homage to Bleriot, 1914
Oil on canvas, 250 x 251.5 cm
Kunstmuseum, Basle, Switzerland

Other works showing movement
- *Champ de Mars: The Red River*, 1911-23
  The Art Institute of Chicago, Chicago, IL, USA
- *Circular Forms*, 1930
  Solomon R. Guggenheim Museum, New York, USA
- *Windows Open Simultaneosly 1st Part, 3rd Motif*, 1912
  Peggy Guggenheim Collection, Guggenheim Museum, Venice, Italy

M C ESCHER (pages 18-19)

(1898-1972) Dutch
Sky and Water I, 1938
Woodcut, 44 x 44 cm
Herbert Palmer Gallery, West Hollywood, CA, USA

Other works showing movement

- ❏ *The Second Day of the Creation*, 1925
  National Gallery of Art, Washington DC, USA
- ❏ *Depth*, 1955
  National Gallery of Canada, Ottawa, Ontario, Canada
- ❏ *Relativity*, 1953
  Gemeentemuseum, The Hague, Brussels

Vincent van GOGH (page 7)

(1853-1890) Dutch
Starry Night, 1889
Oil on canvas, 73 x 92 cm
Museum of Modern Art, New York, NY, USA

Other works showing movement

- ❏ *Wheatfield with Crows*, 1890
  Van Gogh Museum, Amsterdam, Holland
- ❏ *Olive Grove*, 1889
  Kröller-Müller Museum, Otterlo, Holland
- ❏ *Wheatfield with Cypresses*, 1889
  National Gallery, London, UK

Katsushika HOKUSAI (pages 10-11)

(1760-1849) Japanese
The Great Wave off Kanagawa, from the series
'36 Views of Mt.Fuji' (*Fugaku sanjuokkei*) pub.
by Nishimura Eijudo, 1831
Colour woodblock print, 25 x 37.1 cm
Metropolitan Museum of Art, New York, NY, USA

Other works showing movement

- ❏ *Fjiri in Suruga Province*, 1830-33
  British Museum, London, UK
- ❏ *36 Views of Mount Fuji Number 4*,
  Meadows Museum of Art at Centenary College,
  Louisiana, MO, USA
- ❏ *Mitsui Shop, Sugura St, Edo*, 1823-31
  Norton Simon Museum, Pasadena, CA, USA

Jacques-Henri LARTIGUE (page 12)

(1894-1986) French (Corbevoie)
*Grand Prix de l'ACF, automobile Delage,
26 juin 1912*, 1912
Photograph, 16.6 x 23.75 cm
Collection of Madame Lartigue

Other works showing movement

- ❏ *Bouboutte and Louis*, 1910
  Collection of Madame Lartigue
- ❏ *Bichonnade in Flight*, 1905
  Collection of Madame Lartigue
- ❏ *24 Mars*, 1924
  Collection of Madame Lartigue

Etienne-Jules MAREY (page 17)

(1830-1904) French (Beaune)
Fencing Pose, about 1890,
and *Gun Birds*, about 1860
Photographs

Other works showing movement

- ❏ *Man Pole Vaulting*, 1890-91
- ❏ *Figures Geometrique*, 1882-88
- ❏ *Falling Cat*, 1894

Claude MONET (pages 1, 8-9)

(1840-1926) French (Le Harve)
*The Rue Montorgueil, Paris,
30 June 1878*, 1878
Oil on canvas, 81 x 50 cm
Musée D'Orsay, Paris, France

Other works showing movement

- ❏ *Woman with a Parasol*, 1886
  Musée D'Orsay, Paris, France
- ❏ *Wild Coast, Belle-Ile*, 1886
  Musée D'Orsay, Paris, France
- ❏ *Houses of Parliament, London*, 1905
  Musée Marmottan, Paris, France

Edvard MUNCH (page 27)

(1863-1944) Norwegian (Loten)
The Scream, 1893
Tempera on board, 83.5 x 66 cm
Munch Museum, Oslo, Norway

Other works showing movement
❏ *The Dance of Life*
   Munch Museum, Oslo, Norway
❏ *Anxiety*, 1894
   Munch Museum, Oslo, Norway
❏ *The Lonely Ones*, 1899
   Fogg Art Museum, Harvard, Cambridge, MASS, USA

Jackson POLLOCK (pages 14-15)

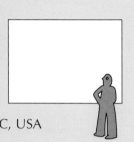

(1912-1956) American (Wyoming)
Lavender Mist No 1, 1950, 1950
Oil, enamel and aluminium on
canvas, 221 x 299.7 cm
National Gallery of Art, Washington DC, USA

Other works showing movement
❏ *Greyed Rainbow*, 1953,
   Art Institute of Chicago, Chicago, IL, USA
❏ *Eyes in the Heat*, 1946,
   Guggenheim Museum, New York, NY, USA
❏ *Blue Poles: Number 11, 1952*, 1952
   National Gallery of Australia, Canberra, Australia

Auguste RODIN (page 21)

(1840-1917) French (Paris)
Dance Movement C (S. 762), 1910-11
Bronze, 36 x 9 x 12 cm
Musée Rodin, Paris, France

Other works showing movement
❏ *Walking Man*, about 1900
   Musée D'Orsay, Paris, France
❏ *The Gates of Hell*, 1880-1917
   Musée Rodin, Paris, France
❏ *Call to Arms*, 1879
   Musée Rodin, Paris, France

Georges SEURAT (pages 4-5)

(1859-1891) French (Paris)
The Circus, 1890-91
Oil on canvas, 182.5 x 147.95 cm
Musée D'Orsay, Paris, France

Other works showing movement
❏ *Le Chahut*, 1889-90
   Kröller-Müller Museum, Otterlo, Holland
❏ *Morning Walk*, 1885
   National Gallery, London, UK
❏ *The Seine at la Grande Jatte*, 1888
   Musée Royaux des Beaux-Art de Belgique, Brussels

JMW TURNER (page 13)

(1775-1851) English (London)
*Rain, Steam and Speed – The Great
Western Railway*, about 1839-44
Oil on canvas, 90.8 x 121.9 cm
National Gallery, London, UK

Other works showing movement
❏ *Snowstorm: Steamboat off a Harbours Mouth,* 1842
   Tate Britain, London, UK
❏ *The Burning of the Houses of Lords and Commons,
   16th October 1834*, 1835
   Philadelphia Museum of Art, Philadelphia, USA
❏ *Slavers throwing Overboard the Dead and Dying –
   Typhoon Coming On ('The Slave Ship')*, 1840,
   Museum of Fine Arts, Boston, MASS, USA

Victor VASARELY (page 24)

1908-1997 French (Hungarian born)
Boo, 1978
Oil on canvas, 200 x 200 cm
Private collection

Other works showing movement
❏ *Vega-Nor*, 1969
   Albright-Knox Art Gallery, Buffalo, New York, NY, USA
❏ *Banya*, 1964
   Tate Britain, London, UK
❏ *Quasar-Fugue*, 1966-73
   Tehran Museum of Contemporary Art, Tehran, Iran

Glossary

Abstract Art that does not try to show things in a real way.

Abstract Expressionism A type of abstract art, also known as 'action painting'.

Apprentice Someone, usually young, who is working for and learning from a skilled person.

Blurred Something that cannot be seen (or heard) clearly.

Bronze A yellowish-brown metal that is a mixture of copper and tin.

Canvas A piece of coarse, stretched cloth on which artists often paint.

Diagonal Having a slanted direction.

Distorted Pulled or twisted out of shape.

Dynamic Having constant movement or change.

Fencing A sport of fighting with blunted swords.

Futurists A group of early twentieth-century Italian artists who portrayed in their art a sense of energy and power of people and objects moving through space.

Graphic Art involving drawing, engraving or lettering.

Illusion A false or unreal picture, idea or belief.

Impasto Paint that has been brushed on thickly, often in layers, to create rough, raised parts.

Impressionists A group of nineteenth-century French painters who liked to paint things they could see with their own eyes, and to capture the effects of movement and light.

Mood The feeling of a painting: such as happy, frightening, exciting, or sad.

Oil paints Thick paints made by mixing ground pigments with oils.

Op Art A form of abstract art that gives the illusion of movement by using pattern and colour.

Optical Relating to the eye, vision and light.

Pattern Objects, shapes or lines that are repeated within a painting or print.

Perspective A method of painting or drawing landscapes, figures and objects to make them appear three-dimensional.

Pointillism A painting technique where an artist uses many small dots of paint to create a picture.

Poses Particular positions of figures in a work of art.

Realistic Showing things in a way that is correct and true to life.

Spheres Solid, round shapes, like balls.

Studio An artist's workplace.

Technique The style in which an artist paints.

Texture The look or feel of the surface of a painting: such as smooth, shiny, rough, or dull.

Woodcut print A print created from a block of wood with a picture cut into it which is then inked and pressed on to a sheet of paper.

Workshop The name for an artist's studio at the time when artists needed assistants to help prepare their paints.

Index

Numbers in **bold** show page numbers of illustrations